INTRODUCTION

Butterflies and moths belong to the second largest order of insects (next to beetles) with approximately 170,000 species worldwide. All have two pairs of wings covered with overlapping layers of fine scales. They feed by uncoiling a long feeding-tube (proboscis) and sucking nutrients from flowers, puddles, etc. When not in use, the tube is coiled under the head.

The two groups differ in several ways:

BUTTERFLIES
- Active by day
- Brightly colored
- Thin body
- Rests with wings held erect over its back
- Antennae are thin and thickened at the tip

MOTHS
- Active at night
- Most are dull colored
- Stout body
- Rests with wings folded, tent-like, over its back.
- Antennae are usually thicker and often feathery

All butterflies and moths have a complex life cycle consisting of four developmental stages.

1. **EGGS** – Eggs are laid singly or in clusters on vegetation or on the ground. One or more clutches of eggs may be laid each year.
2. **CATERPILLARS (LARVAE)** – These worm-like creatures hatch from eggs and feed primarily on plants (often on the host plant on which the eggs were laid). As they grow, larvae shed their skin periodically.
3. **PUPAE** – Pupae are the 'cases' within which caterpillars transform into adults. The pupa of a butterfly is known as a chrysalis; those of moths are called cocoons. In cooler regions, pupae often over-winter before maturing into butterflies or moths.
4. **ADULT** – Butterflies/moths emerge from pupae to feed and breed.

ATTRACTING BUTTERFLIES TO YOUR YARD

1. **Food** – Almost all butterfly caterpillars eat plants; adult butterflies feed almost exclusively on plant nectar. Your local garden shop, library and bookstore will have information on which plants attract specific species.
2. **Water** – Soak the soil in your garden or sandy areas to create puddles. These provide a source of water and minerals.
3. **Rocks** – Put large flat rocks in sunny areas. Butterflies will gather there to spread their wings and warm up.
4. **Brush** – Small brush piles and hollow logs provide ideal places for butterflies to lay their eggs and hibernate over the winter.

Most illustrations show the upper wings of males unless otherwise noted. The measurements denote the wingspan of species. Note that wing shape differs in flight and at rest. Illustrations are not to scale.

Text and illustrations © 2020 by Waterford Press Inc. All rights reserved.
Cover images © Shutterstock.
To order, call 800-434-2555.
For permissions, or to share comments, e-mail editor@waterfordpress.com
For information on custom-published products, call 800-434-2555 or e-mail info@waterfordpress.com

Waterford Press produces reference guides that introduce novices to nature, science, travel and languages. Product information is featured on the website:
www.waterfordpress.com

Made in the USA

$7.95 U.S.

ISBN 978-1-62005-386-7

50795

9 781620 053867

8 84682 01371 4

10 9 8 7 6 5 4 3 2 1   202402

WISCONSIN BUTTERFLIES & POLLINATORS

WISCONSIN BUTTERFLIES & POLLINATORS   Kavanagh/Leung

A Folding Pocket Guide to Familiar Species

T0123984

SWALLOWTAILS & ALLIES

This Family includes the largest butterfly species. Most are colorful and have a tail-like projection on each hindwing.

Eastern Tiger Swallowtail
Papilio glaucus
To 6 in. (15 cm)

Giant Swallowtail
Papilio cresphontes
To 6 in. (15 cm)
One of the largest North American butterflies.

Black Swallowtail
Papilio polyxenes To 3.5 in. (9 cm)
Note two rows of yellow spots on forewings and orange spots on hindwings.

Canadian Tiger Swallowtail
Papilio canadensis
To 3 in. (8 cm)
A smaller version of the eastern tiger swallowtail.

WHITES & SULPHURS

White and yellow/orange butterflies are among the first to appear in spring.

Mustard White
Artogeia oleracea To 2 in. (5 cm)
Common in moist forests. Feeds on a variety of mustards.

Cabbage White
Pieris rapae To 2 in. (5 cm)
One of the most common butterflies. Feeds on cabbage leaves and wild mustards.

Olympia Marble
Euchloe olympia
To 1.5 in. (4 cm)
Common in open areas and along lakeshores.

Checkered White
Pontia protodice
To 1.75 in. (4.5 cm)

WHITES & SULPHURS

West Virginia White
Artogeia virginiensis
To 2.25 in. (5.2 cm)
Springtime butterfly inhabits moist woodlands.

Little Yellow
Eurema lisa
To 1.5 in. (4 cm)
Note small size.

Pink-edged Sulphur
Colias interior
To 1.75 in. (4.2 cm)

Clouded Sulphur
Colias philodice To 2 in. (5 cm)
Common in open areas and along roadsides.

Orange Sulphur
Colias eurytheme
To 2 in. (6 cm)
Gold-orange butterfly has a prominent forewing spot.

Dainty Sulphur
Nathalis iole
To 1.25 in. (3.2 cm)

GOSSAMER-WINGED BUTTERFLIES

This family of small butterflies often have small, hair-like tails on its hindwings. Many rest with their wings folded and underwings exposed.

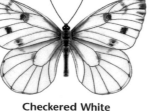

Spring Azure
Celastrina ladon To 1.25 in. (3.2 cm)
Common May to July.

Summer Azure
Celastrina neglecta
To 1 in. (3 cm)
Common in June to August.

GOSSAMER-WINGED BUTTERFLIES

Underwings

Silvery Blue
Glaucopsyche lygdamus To 1.25 in. (3.2 cm)
Wings are gray below with a line of dark spots along the wing margin.

Eastern Tailed Blue
Cupido comyntas To 1 in. (3 cm)
Note orange spots above thread-like hindwing tails.

Purplish Copper
Epidemia helloides
To 1.5 in. (4 cm)
Purplish sheen is most evident in bright sunlight.

American Copper
Lycaena phlaeas
To 1.25 in. (3.2 cm)
Common in disturbed areas and along roadsides.

Harvester
Feniseca tarquinius
To 1.25 in. (3.2 cm)
North America's only carnivorous butterfly feeds primarily on aphids.

Brown Elfin
Incisalia augustinus
To 1 in. (3 cm)
Underwings are chocolate-brown.

Bronze Copper
Hyllolycaena hyllus To 2 in. (5 cm)
Common in wet meadows and near waterways.

Coral Hairstreak
Harkenclenus titus
To 1.5 in. (4 cm)
Note reddish spots along margin of hindwings. Upperwings are brownish.

Underwings

GOSSAMER-WINGED BUTTERFLIES

Underwings

Gray Hairstreak
Strymon melinus
To 1.25 in. (3.2 cm)
Dark greyish butterfly has orange spots on hindwings. Upperwings are brownish.

Underwings

Banded Hairstreak
Satyrium calanus
To 1.25 in. (3.2 cm)
Rests with wings folded and underwings exposed. Upperwings are brownish.

SKIPPERS

Named for their fast, bouncing flight, skippers have distinctive antennae that end in curved clubs.

Arctic Skipper
Carterocephalus palaemon
To 1 in. (3 cm)

Hobomok Skipper
Poanes hobomok
To 1.5 in. (4 cm)

Common Sootywing
Pholisora catullus
To 1.25 in. (3.2 cm)
Forewings have two curved rows of white spots. Found in open and disturbed areas.

Fiery Skipper
Hylephila phyleus
To 1.5 in. (4 cm)
Active during the day, they feed on flower nectar in gardens and fields.

Underwings

Silver-spotted Skipper
Epargyreus clarus To 2.5 in. (6 cm)
Has a large, irregular silver patch on the underside of its hindwings. Patch is absent on the forewings.

Northern Cloudywing
Thorybes pylades
To 1.75 in. (4.5 cm)
Common in open areas near flowers and mud puddles.

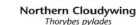

BRUSHFOOTS

This Family is named for its small forelegs that they use to 'taste' food.

Milbert's Tortoiseshell
Aglais milberti To 2 in. (5 cm)

Viceroy
Limenitis archippus
To 3 in. (8 cm)
Told from similar monarch by its smaller size and the thin, black band on its hindwings.

White Admiral
Limenitis arthemis
To 3 in. (8 cm)
Common in upland deciduous forests.

Mourning Cloak
Nymphalis antiopa
To 3.5 in. (9 cm)
Emerges during the first spring thaw. Found in a variety of habitats.

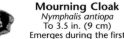

Compton Tortoiseshell
Nymphalis vau-album
To 3 in. (8 cm)
Note ragged wings.

Hackberry Emperor
Asterocampa celtis
To 2.5 in. (6 cm)
Is gray-brown to orange.

Pearl Crescent
Phyciodes tharos
To 1.5 in. (4 cm)
Note black margins on wings. Hindwing is marked with dark crescent-shaped spots.

Northern Crescent
Phyciodes cocyta
To 1.5 in. (4 cm)

BRUSHFOOTS

Monarch
Danaus plexippus
To 4 in. (10 cm)
Note rows of white spots on edges of wings. Annual migration covers thousands of miles.

Eyed Brown
Satyrodes eurydice To 2 in. (5 cm)
Note 4 spots on forewings and 6 spots on hindwings.

Little Wood Satyr
Megisto cymela To 2 in. (5 cm)
Note 2 eyespots on each wing.

Common Wood Nymph
Cercyonis pegala
To 3 in. (8 cm)
Note 2 eyespots on the forewing. Yellow band is not always present.

Buckeye
Junonia coenia
To 2.5 in. (6 cm)
Note orange wing bars on forewings and eight distinct eyespots.

Northern Pearly-eye
Enodia anthedon
To 2 in. (5 cm)
Common in clearings and deciduous woodlands.

Question Mark
Polygonia interrogationis
To 2.5 in. (6 cm)
Note lilac margin on wings. Underwings feature a silvery patch that resembles a question mark on the hindwing.

Eastern Comma
Polygonia comma
To 2 in. (5 cm)
Note ragged wing margins. Has a silvery comma mark on the underside of its hindwings.

BRUSHFOOTS

Meadow Fritillary
Clossiana bellona
To 2 in. (5 cm)
Found in meadows and along streams and hillsides.

Great Spangled Fritillary
Speyeria cybele
To 3 in. (8 cm)
Common in marshes and wet meadows.

Red Admiral
Vanessa atalanta
To 2.5 in. (6 cm)
Dark butterfly has prominent orange bars on forewings and border of hindwings.

Red-spotted Purple
Limenitis arthemis astyanax
To 3.5 in. (9 cm)

American Lady
Vanessa virginiensis To 2 in. (5 cm)
Underside of hindwings feature prominent eyespots.

American Snout
Libytheana carinenta
To 2 in. (5 cm)
Snout is formed from projecting mouth parts that enclose its coiled proboscis.

Painted Lady
Vanessa cardui To 2.5 in. (6 cm)
Tip of forewing is dark with white spots. Underwings have four iridescent blue-black spots on the hindwing.

Baltimore Checkerspot
Euphydryas phaeton
To 2.5 in. (6 cm)

MOTHS

Hummingbird Clearwing
Hemaris thysbe To 2 in. (5 cm)
Wings have clear patches. Hovers near flowers like a hummingbird.

Cabbage Looper
Trichoplusia ni To 1.5 in. (4 cm)
Named for the behavior of the caterpillar which 'inches' forward with an arched back as it moves.

Cecropia Moth
Hyalophora cecropia To 6 in. (15 cm)
Note white, crescent-shaped marks on hindwings.

Luna Moth
Actias luna
To 4.5 in. (11 cm)

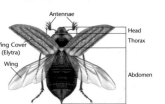

White-lined Sphinx
Hyles lineata To 3.5 in. (9 cm)
Active at all hours, it hovers like a hummingbird. Caterpillar has a 'horn' at its rear.

Fall Webworm Moth
Hyphantria cunea
To 1.5 in. (4 cm)
Larvae live in a communal web and attack over 100 species of trees.

Webworm Web

Eastern Tent Caterpillar Moth
Malacosoma americanum
To 1.5 in. (4 cm)
Communal web nests are a common sight in fruit trees in spring.

Tent Caterpillar Web

Polyphemus Moth
Antheraea polyphemus
To 6 in. (15 cm)

OTHER POLLINATORS

About 75% of the crop plants grown worldwide depend on pollinators – bees, butterflies, birds, bats and other animals – for fertilization and reproduction. Although some species of plants are pollinated by the wind and water, the vast majority (almost 90%) need the help of animals to act as pollinating agents. More than 1,000 of the world's most important foods, beverages and medicines are derived from plants that require pollination by animals.

Pollinating animals worldwide are threatened due to loss of habitat, introduced and invasive species, pesticides, diseases and parasites.

Bees, Wasps & Flies

North America is home to approximately 4,000 species of bees. Of these, the most important crop pollinators are wild native honey bees and managed colonies of European honey bees. Other important flying insects include bumble bees, mason bees, carpenter bees, wasps and numerous flies. With honey bee populations in huge decline due certain illnesses and habitat loss, this can have a huge impact on food production in North America.

HONEY BEE ANATOMY

Beetles

The living jewels of the bug world, beetles are the dominant life group on the earth with about 400,000 species found in all habitats except the polar regions and the oceans. They are invaluable to ecosystems as both pollinators and scavengers, feeding on dead animals and fallen trees to recycle nutrients back into the soil. Some, however, are serious pests and cause great harm to living plants (trees, crops). Learn to recognize the good from the bad and involve your local land management and pest control resources to mitigate the spread of harmful beetles.

BEETLE ANATOMY

Birds, Bats & Other Animals

50+ species of North American birds occasionally feed on plant nectar and blossoms, but it is the primary food source for hummingbirds and orioles. Sugar water feeders are a good way to supplement the energy of nectar-drinkers, but it is far better to plant flowers and shrubs that provide native sources of nutrient-rich nectar. While very common in tropical climates around the world, only three species of nectar feeding bats are found in the southwestern U.S. They are important pollinators of desert plants including large cacti (organ pipe, saguaro), agaves and century plants. Rodents, lizards and small mammals like mice also pollinate plants when feeding on their nectar and flower heads.

Ruby-throated Hummingbird

Long-nosed Bat

OTHER POLLINATORS

Attracting Bees & Other Pollinators

- Recognize the pollinators in your area and plant gardens to support the larvae and adults of different species.
- Cultivate native pollen and nectar-producing plants that bloom at different times throughout the growing season. Ensure the species you select will thrive with the amount of sunshine and moisture at the site. Reduce/eliminate use of pesticides. If you use any type of repellent, ensure it is organic and pesticide free.
- The plants that attract birds, butterflies and moths for pollination most commonly have bright red, orange or yellow flowers with very little scent. Butterflies prefer flat-topped "cluster" flowers. Hummingbirds prefer tube or funnel-shaped flowers.
- Create areas, out of the sun, where pollinators can rest and avoid predation while foraging.
- Supply water for both drinking and bathing. Create shallow puddles for bees & butterflies.
- Create nesting boxes or brushy areas that provide protection from predation and are suitable for pollinators to raise their young.
- Learn to recognize the good and bad garden bugs.

CATERPILLARS

Tiger Swallowtail

Giant Swallowtail

Mourning Cloak

Great Spangled Fritillary

Sulphur

Monarch

Buckeye

Skipper

White-lined Sphinx

Painted Lady

Fall Webworm Moth

Cabbage Looper

Tent Caterpillar Moth